THIS BOOK BELONGS TO:

CONTACT INFORMATION	
NAME:	
ADDRESS:	
PHONE:	

START / END DATES

___ / ___ / _____   TO   ___ / ___ / _____

This Baby Memory Book is dedicated to all the parents out there who want to keep track of their baby's memories and document their findings in the process.

You are my inspiration for producing books and I'm honored to be a part of keeping all of your baby memory notes and records organized.

This journal notebook will help you record your baby's memories.

Thoughtfully put together with these sections to record: Photos or Souvenir, Date, Age, and Today's Memory.

How to Use this Book

The purpose of this book is to keep all of your Baby's Memory notes all in one place. It will help keep you organized.

This Baby Memory Book will allow you to accurately document every detail about your child's first years.

Here are examples of the prompts for you to fill in and write about your experience in this book:

1. Photo or Souvenir - A place to attach photos or a souvenir.

2. Date - Write the date.

3. Age - Record how old your baby is on this date.

4. Today's Memory - Blank lined space to document and writing details of your baby's memory, your personal thoughts, etc.

Baby Memory Journal

DATE:

AGE:

TODAY'S MEMORY

Baby Memory Journal

DATE: AGE:

TODAY'S MEMORY

Baby Memory Journal

DATE:

AGE:

TODAY'S MEMORY

Baby Memory Journal

DATE: AGE:

TODAY'S MEMORY

Baby Memory Journal

DATE: AGE:

TODAY'S MEMORY

Baby Memory Journal

DATE:

AGE:

TODAY'S MEMORY

Baby Memory Journal

DATE:

AGE:

TODAY'S MEMORY

Baby Memory Journal

DATE:

AGE:

TODAY'S MEMORY

Baby Memory Journal

DATE: AGE:

TODAY'S MEMORY

Baby Memory Journal

DATE:

AGE:

TODAY'S MEMORY

Baby Memory Journal

DATE: AGE:

TODAY'S MEMORY

Baby Memory Journal

DATE: AGE:

TODAY'S MEMORY

Baby Memory Journal

DATE:

AGE:

TODAY'S MEMORY

Baby Memory Journal

DATE:

AGE:

TODAY'S MEMORY

Baby Memory Journal

DATE:

AGE:

TODAY'S MEMORY

Baby Memory Journal

DATE: _____   AGE: _____

TODAY'S MEMORY

Baby Memory Journal

DATE:

AGE:

TODAY'S MEMORY

Baby Memory Journal

DATE:

AGE:

TODAY'S MEMORY

Baby Memory Journal

DATE:

AGE:

TODAY'S MEMORY

Baby Memory Journal

DATE:

AGE:

TODAY'S MEMORY

Baby Memory Journal

DATE:

AGE:

TODAY'S MEMORY

Baby Memory Journal

DATE: AGE:

TODAY'S MEMORY

Baby Memory Journal

DATE:

AGE:

TODAY'S MEMORY

Baby Memory Journal

DATE: AGE:

TODAY'S MEMORY

Baby Memory Journal

DATE:

AGE:

TODAY'S MEMORY

Baby Memory Journal

DATE:

AGE:

TODAY'S MEMORY

Baby Memory Journal

DATE: AGE:

TODAY'S MEMORY

Baby Memory Journal

DATE:

AGE:

TODAY'S MEMORY

Baby Memory Journal

DATE:

AGE:

TODAY'S MEMORY

Baby Memory Journal

DATE: AGE:

TODAY'S MEMORY

Baby Memory Journal

DATE:

AGE:

TODAY'S MEMORY

Baby Memory Journal

DATE:

AGE:

TODAY'S MEMORY

Baby Memory Journal

DATE:

AGE:

TODAY'S MEMORY

Baby Memory Journal

DATE:

AGE:

TODAY'S MEMORY

Baby Memory Journal

DATE:

AGE:

TODAY'S MEMORY

Baby Memory Journal

DATE:

AGE:

TODAY'S MEMORY

Baby Memory Journal

DATE: _____ AGE: _____

TODAY'S MEMORY

Baby Memory Journal

DATE:

AGE:

TODAY'S MEMORY

Baby Memory Journal

DATE:

AGE:

TODAY'S MEMORY

Baby Memory Journal

DATE:　　　　　　　　　　　　　　　　　　　　AGE:

TODAY'S MEMORY

Baby Memory Journal

DATE:

AGE:

TODAY'S MEMORY

Baby Memory Journal

DATE:

AGE:

TODAY'S MEMORY

Baby Memory Journal

DATE:

AGE:

TODAY'S MEMORY

Baby Memory Journal

DATE:

AGE:

TODAY'S MEMORY

Baby Memory Journal

DATE: _____ AGE: _____

TODAY'S MEMORY

Baby Memory Journal

DATE: AGE:

TODAY'S MEMORY

Baby Memory Journal

DATE:

AGE:

TODAY'S MEMORY

Baby Memory Journal

DATE: AGE:

TODAY'S MEMORY

Baby Memory Journal

DATE: AGE:

TODAY'S MEMORY

Baby Memory Journal

DATE:

AGE:

TODAY'S MEMORY

Baby Memory Journal

DATE:

AGE:

TODAY'S MEMORY

Baby Memory Journal

DATE:

AGE:

TODAY'S MEMORY

Baby Memory Journal

DATE:

AGE:

TODAY'S MEMORY

Baby Memory Journal

DATE:

AGE:

TODAY'S MEMORY

Baby Memory Journal

DATE: AGE:

TODAY'S MEMORY

Baby Memory Journal

DATE:

AGE:

TODAY'S MEMORY

Baby Memory Journal

DATE:

AGE:

TODAY'S MEMORY

Baby Memory Journal

DATE: AGE:

TODAY'S MEMORY

Baby Memory Journal

DATE: AGE:

TODAY'S MEMORY

Baby Memory Journal

DATE: _____ AGE: _____

TODAY'S MEMORY

Baby Memory Journal

DATE:

AGE:

TODAY'S MEMORY

Baby Memory Journal

DATE:

AGE:

TODAY'S MEMORY

Baby Memory Journal

DATE: _____   AGE: _____

TODAY'S MEMORY

_____
_____
_____
_____
_____
_____
_____
_____
_____
_____
_____

Baby Memory Journal

DATE:

AGE:

TODAY'S MEMORY

Baby Memory Journal

DATE: _____ AGE: _____

TODAY'S MEMORY

Baby Memory Journal

DATE:

AGE:

TODAY'S MEMORY

Baby Memory Journal

DATE: _____ AGE: _____

TODAY'S MEMORY

Baby Memory Journal

DATE:

AGE:

TODAY'S MEMORY

Baby Memory Journal

DATE:

AGE:

TODAY'S MEMORY

Baby Memory Journal

DATE:

AGE:

TODAY'S MEMORY

Baby Memory Journal

DATE:

AGE:

TODAY'S MEMORY

Baby Memory Journal

DATE:

AGE:

TODAY'S MEMORY

Baby Memory Journal

DATE:

AGE:

TODAY'S MEMORY

Baby Memory Journal

DATE: AGE:

TODAY'S MEMORY

Baby Memory Journal

DATE:

AGE:

TODAY'S MEMORY

Baby Memory Journal

DATE:

AGE:

TODAY'S MEMORY

Baby Memory Journal

DATE: AGE:

TODAY'S MEMORY

Baby Memory Journal

DATE:

AGE:

TODAY'S MEMORY

Baby Memory Journal

DATE:

AGE:

TODAY'S MEMORY

Baby Memory Journal

DATE:

AGE:

TODAY'S MEMORY

Baby Memory Journal

DATE: AGE:

TODAY'S MEMORY

Baby Memory Journal

DATE: AGE:

TODAY'S MEMORY

Baby Memory Journal

DATE:

AGE:

TODAY'S MEMORY

Baby Memory Journal

DATE: _____   AGE: _____

TODAY'S MEMORY

Baby Memory Journal

DATE:

AGE:

TODAY'S MEMORY

Baby Memory Journal

DATE:

AGE:

TODAY'S MEMORY

Baby Memory Journal

DATE: AGE:

TODAY'S MEMORY

Baby Memory Journal

DATE: AGE:

TODAY'S MEMORY

Baby Memory Journal

DATE:

AGE:

TODAY'S MEMORY

Baby Memory Journal

DATE:

AGE:

TODAY'S MEMORY

Baby Memory Journal

DATE:

AGE:

TODAY'S MEMORY

Baby Memory Journal

DATE:

AGE:

TODAY'S MEMORY

Baby Memory Journal

DATE: AGE:

TODAY'S MEMORY

Baby Memory Journal

DATE:

AGE:

TODAY'S MEMORY

Baby Memory Journal

DATE:

AGE:

TODAY'S MEMORY

Baby Memory Journal

DATE:

AGE:

TODAY'S MEMORY

Baby Memory Journal

DATE:

AGE:

TODAY'S MEMORY